Self-Esteem Enhancers

PROVIDENCE HOUSE PUBLISHERS
Franklin, Tennessee

Self-Esteem Enhancers

Inner-Directed Guidelines for Successful Living

Virgie M. Binford

Dorothy N. Cowling

Printed in the United States of America

03   02   01   00   99   1   2   3   4   5

Library of Congress Catalog Card Number: 99-66910

ISBN: 1-57736-166-0

Cover design by Gary Bozeman

PROVIDENCE HOUSE PUBLISHERS
238 Seaboard Lane • Franklin, Tennessee 37067
800-321-5692
www.providencehouse.com

For all of the lives we have been blessed to touch in numerous positive ways, including our families and career development affiliates.

For all of the interested people who continue to strive to improve life chances for children and families.

May you be inspired and motivated to enhance your self-esteem and share your gems of wisdom to build will and skill to lift others as you climb the ladder of success.

CONTENTS

Within each individual lies the seeds of success. Conceiving, believing, and achieving will generate plants and fruit for a bountiful harvest of ideas for personal growth.

—Binford and Cowling

FOREWORD

Having served for twelve years as international president of Pi Lambda Theta, an international honor society and professional association in education, and having held several other offices on state and local levels, I am convinced that healthy self-esteem is crucial to success in every area of life.

Interacting with authors Virgie M. Binford, international vice-president, and Dorothy N. Cowling, past president of the Virginia area chapter of Pi Lambda Theta, I am impressed with their contributions as self-esteem enchancers in numerous global activities that promote excellence in the process of education.

Their success stories in teaching and learning from preschool to university levels have earned them exemplary status in guiding the growth and development of individuals and multicultural and multiethnic groups.

As role models of healthy self-esteemers, they have collaborated in sharing gems of wisdom that will provide a blueprint for readers to emulate in self-development and strategies for inspiring others to set and achieve goals for successful living in all areas of life.

My membership and participation in the National Association of Self-Esteem made this publication of great interest to me. Serving as an educational consultant, I have assumed the responsibility of planning, implementing, and monitoring self-esteem conferences in Hawaii and Virginia.

Binford and Cowling have served as resource persons through the years, sharing esteeming ideas for excellence in education and exemplary practices.

As a former teacher, educational specialist, and school administrator, I am cognizant of the importance of the need for self-esteem enhancers.

Frances Shimotsu,
International President
Pi Lambda Theta Honor Society and
Professional Association in Education

PREFACE

During several generations as teachers and learners, we have developed and shared acts of gratitude through our educational careers, which have spanned the globe in both rural and urban areas. We have actualized a mentor-mentee relationship for a period of more than fifty years, beginning as a student and a school administrator at Virginia State College. Self-esteem enhancing became part and parcel of our daily vocabulary and our activities.

Throughout the years we have set and achieved numerous goals that increased our knowledge, skills, and creativity as we utilized coping skills to overcome obstacles and adversities in life.

This publication is a blueprint of strategies that have worked for us and for thousands of individuals of all ethnic and cultural backgrounds whom we have interacted with in school, community, and faith settings. Feedback from various age groups, ranging from preschoolers to senior citizens, convinced us that our self-esteem enhancing model is worth replicating to larger audiences. Through collaboration in planning, implementing, and evaluating results of our work, we developed this book to share our gems of wisdom with readers. May you find your own inner-winning spirit of faith, hope, and unconditional love.

ACKNOWLEDGMENTS

Our indebtedness for guidance, support, and positive reinforcement that empowered us to write this publication goes to countless numbers of family members, friends, instructors, consultants, and to our Creator who continues to surround us with positive attitudes and actions to serve as role models for all mankind.

Through the years, our training and development by great minds built sturdy bridges of faith, hope, love, and "can do" attitudes that keep us focused on the importance of stretching our minds to new horizons. While we are unable to recall the names of all who provided us with encouragement and strong shoulders to lean on, we acknowledge their help in making this publication possible.

Self-Esteem Enhancers

EFFECTIVE ENHANCERS
ARE CONNECTORS OF

MIND, BODY, SOUL

SEE AND REMEMBER
DO AND UNDERSTAND
IN AN ATTITUDE OF GRATITUDE

INTRODUCTION

Over years of interacting with diverse groups and individuals ranging from preschoolers to adults, we have encountered far too many who have refused to succeed in achieving tasks because of an "I can't" or "I am unwilling to try" for fear of failure. On the other hand, we have observed many from similar backgrounds who succeeded because they adopted an "I can" attitude and were willing to try.

After sharing our perceptions and discussing our observations with many people who exhibited high achievement as well as those whose achievements were minimal, we have come to believe that healthy high self-esteem made the difference.

Our definition of self-esteem is the "inner-winning" spirit that propels one toward positive action for success in achieving predetermined goals. It is action that is fueled with enthusiasm and determination to set realistic goals and achieve them in spite of adversities and stumbling blocks.

Information in this book, along with successful practices of many high self-esteemers, will, hopefully, serve as tools for continuous improvements to develop and maintain positive attitudes toward self and others. Suggestions for planning, implementing, and monitoring a desirable blueprint are shared. Guidelines for coping with challenges that obstruct the structures of faith, hope, and unconditional love are outlined.

Testimonials of persons having made use of self-esteem builders are included as documentation of the power to change from negative to positive behavior.

Powerhouses of inner selves will become illuminated with increasing bank accounts of possibilities in goal setting and achievement in every area of life for every age group and for varying levels of competencies.

Our objectives include inspiring readers and stimulating their thinking skills to make creativity

> OUR DEFINITION OF SELF-ESTEEM IS THE "INNER-WINNING" SPIRIT THAT PROPELS ONE TOWARD POSITIVE ACTION FOR SUCCESS IN ACHIEVING PREDETERMINED GOALS

an integral part of dreams, desires, and determination in setting and achieving goals.

Ten chapters serve as interest grabbers that provide affirmations for a foundation for building resiliency. Strategies are shared suggesting how to turn obstacles into opportunities to become self-reliant and change the lemons of strife into the lemonade of peace and prosperity.

SEEK THE BEST

BELIEVE THE BEST

WORK FOR THE BEST

EXPECT THE BEST

BE THE BEST

AND

ENJOY THE BEST

Chapter One

SEARCH FOR IDEAS TO STIMULATE INTEREST IN SELF-IMPROVEMENT

 The importance of ideas was crystallized in these words of Theodore Dostoyevsky: "Neither man nor nation can exist without a sublime idea." William Shakespeare illuminated the relevance of ideas by stating that they are "the very coinage of your brain."

Sources of ideas are abundant. They are ripe and ready to be plucked from various streams of information, from firsthand utilization of actual experiences to vicarious data derived from written words and the media.

Some meditators boast about the number of ideas that are revealed to them in periods of silence when introspection is operating at its highest peak.

Some dreamers claim that ideas surface as visions when they spring forth in the realm between sleep and wakefulness. They reassure us that this state of restfulness is pregnant with ideas waiting to be born into a state of reality.

Studies of biographies and autobiographies contain ideas, in many instances, that whet the appetite for model self-improvement success stories.

Testimonies from several people who were interviewed by the authors indicated that the adversity of losing their jobs through downsizing, reorganization, and other reasons forced them to go through introspective periods of prayer, meditation, and other forms of spiritual renewal that revealed ideas and the mandate given by our Master Teacher, Jesus, who declared: "Ask and it will be given to you; seek and you will find; knock and the door will be opened to you. For everyone who asks receives; he who seeks finds; and to him who knocks, the door will be opened" (Matt. 7:7–8 NIV).

SEARCHING FOR IDEAS IS MANDATORY FOR SELF-IMPROVEMENT

Searching for ideas is mandatory for self-improvement. It indicates that one believes there are answers to questions of concern, there are solutions to problems, and there are coping skills for challenges.

The word "idea" is derived from the Greek meaning of "to see." If we are to elevate faith in ourselves and build an inner-winning spirit, we must be able to see opportunities for success in chaotic conditions. We must be able to do what some of our forefathers and foremothers advocated—look through muddy water and spy dry land.

Once ideas are crystallized, action must be executed to produce end results that accompany goal-setting decision making and ensure self-improvement!

FUEL YOUR LIFE

WITH

POSITIVE ENERGY OF DIVINE FAITH

ILLUMINATED HOPE

AND

UNCONDITIONAL LOVE

FOR

ALL MANKIND

Chapter Two

ENERGIZE YOUR LIFE WITH POSITIVE AFFIRMATIONS

Affirmations are the expressions of goals that are visualized through imagination as if they have already been realized. According to Shakti Gawain in the *Creative Visualization Workbook* (1995), "The process includes picking a goal that you desire. State it in a simple sentence, in the present tense, as if it were already true." For example, "I am healthy, happy, and terrific." Positive affirmations empower people to be whatever they desire through the use of the imagination, earnest concentration, and visualization of the end result as positive outcomes. Positive affirmations make use of visions to promote achievement in all areas of life.

Jonathan Swift defined "vision" as "the art of seeing things invisible." We are convinced that visions are important in building self-esteem as caring, concerned, and committed creatures with a rightful place on earth, of worth to ourselves and to all mankind. If we neglect this important aspect of life we are doing an injustice to our status as vital parts of the universe. Recalling that the Holy Bible affirms that "where there is no vision, the people perish," we are mandated to use our three pounds of brain power to stimulate desire, and visualize and affirm that we are created to be successful in every area of life.

SOWING SEEDS OF POSITIVE AFFIRMATIONS . . . ENABLES US TO REAP THE HARVEST OF POSITIVE THOUGHTS AND POSITIVE ACTIONS

Comprehensive affirmations should be utilized to help develop our maximum potential in areas of health (both physical and mental), career development choices, home and family relationships, spiritual and ethical values, financial security, and social and cultural awareness.

Sowing seeds of positive affirmations on a daily basis enables us to reap the harvest of positive thoughts and positive actions. The following positive affirmations, as starter uppers, can be spoken and written in a journal at least twice daily as a beginning step toward realizing their achievement:

- I am enjoying good health and peace of mind.
- My memory is effective for recalling pertinent information.
- My career is productive with daily satisfaction.
- I have unconditional love for my home and family.
- My spiritual renewal and ethical values are producing an inner-winning attitude in all areas of life.
- I am secure with meeting my financial obligations on time.
- My social interaction and respect of cultural diversity are excellent.

Add additional affirmations to this list and make necessary changes to meet your unique needs and interests. Believe that the affirmations are real and they will come true. One writer affirmed that "whatever the mind can conceive and believe, it can achieve."

ENERGIZING ONE'S LIFE WITH POSITIVE AFFIRMATIONS . . . WILL BRING INNER PEACE

Energizing one's life with positive affirmations, which serve as activators to increase knowledge, skills, and creativity, will bring inner peace and form a climate where mind, body, and soul can experience joy and contentment.

In Wayne Dyer's book, *You'll See It When You Believe It,* some characteristics of inner peace are listed as follows:

A tendency to think and act spontaneously rather than on fears based on past experiences

An unmistakable ability to enjoy each moment

A loss of interest in judging people

A loss of interest in interpreting the actions of others

A loss of interest in conflict

A loss of the ability to worry

Frequent overwhelming episodes of appreciation

Contented feelings of connectedness with others and nature

Frequent attacks of smiling

An increased susceptibility to the love extended by others as well as the uncontrollable urge to extend it

These suggestions have been tested and proven to be workable in the lives of numerous people with whom we have interacted over several decades. They came from diversified backgrounds and represented multicultural and multiethnic groups. Yet, there has been common consent that positive energy results from concerted efforts made to accept self as a biological wonder and to believe in the power to think, act, and produce worthy deeds.

UNCONDITIONAL LOVE
WILL OPEN
DOORS OF SUCCESS
THAT NO ONE
CAN CLOSE

Chapter Three

LOVE SELF AND OTHERS UNCONDITIONALLY

 In sharing the need for expressing unconditional love, William Wordsworth stated, "The best portion of a good man's life is his little, nameless, unremembered acts of kindness and of love."

A mandate in the Holy Bible is a great reminder of the supremacy of unconditional love: "Let all that you do be done in love" (1 Cor. 16:14).

The timeless advice of Martin Luther King Jr. demonstrated the importance he placed on the power of unconditional love: "Along the way of life, someone must have sense enough and morality enough to cut off the chain of hate. This can only be done by projecting the ethic of love to the center of our lives."

Another reason for demonstrating unconditional love is found in 1 John 4:11, which states, "since God so loved us, we also ought to love one another."

A recipe for enhancing the process of love was shared in this verse by Edwin Markham:

He drew a circle that shut me out—
　　Heretic rebel, a thing to flout.
But love and I had the wit to win—
　　We drew a circle that took him in.

In illuminating the importance of love as a passport to happiness, Victor Hugo stated, "The supreme happiness of life is the conviction that we are loved—loved for ourselves; nay rather, loved in spite of ourselves."

The healing power of love was communicated by Karl Meninger in this declaration: "Love is the medicine for the sickness of the world."

Robert Browning expounded the powerful force of love in this message: "Take away love and our earth is a tomb."

Charles Dickens, recognizing love as a center of survival, declared that "a loving heart is the truest wisdom."

Three significant gifts of mankind are illustrated in the phrase "faith, hope and love." The phrase concludes with this wisdom: "but the greatest of these is love" (1 Cor. 13:13).

Throughout the ages, unconditional love has proven to be a force to strengthen the weak, to prove help for the helpless, to be a comforter for the fearful, to be a healer for the sick, to be a home for the homeless, to be food for the hungry and water for the thirsty, to provide education for the illiterate, to be a solace for distress, and to be a savior for sinners.

When love is unconditional, it is a stupendous power for survival. Unconditional love for self and others will be illuminated when there is a storehouse of survival skills and coping strategies. Becoming an "inner winner" in all areas of life will result from a sincere desire to practice self-accetance and acceptance of all people as worthy of a rightful place on planet Earth. The beginning point is a genuine love of self as one who is created in the image of God.

> WHEN LOVE IS UNCONDITIONAL, IT IS A STUPENDOUS POWER FOR SURVIVAL

Leo Buscaglia, in his book *Bus 9 to Paradise*, shares many ideas for creating one's own paradise through the development of a positive attitude toward self and others. He suggests in vivid details throughout this volume that true love will become evident for self and all other human beings when there is determination to celebrate life with a passion as a birthright of joy and stupendous wonder in divine nature.

Those who consider themselves effective "people builders" in any area, including the home, school, workplace, and community, must engage in teaching people the importance of loving self and others unconditionally. In his publication, *Power Secrets of Managing People*, Rice described the "how" and "why" of giving people a feeling of self-satisfaction and self-admiration of beauty and inner peace. He stated that in bestowing authority and responsibility for generating unconditional love "you lit the fire of self-esteem, of enthusiasm and of motivation toward your mutual goals" (p. 129).

In developing personal strengths of people, Garfield offers these attributes of self-development in *Peak Performers*:

- Missions that motivate
- Self-management through self-mastery
- Results in real time
- Team building/team playing
- Course correction
- Change management

Briley offers "the secret of positive thinkers' success" in his publication, *Are You Positive?* He amplifies the text that is pertinent to the importance of possessing unconditional love for self and others by stressing the importance of "Positive Goals" picturing with these gems of wisdom:

What we visualize, we tend to do or become.

Failure images in the mind can only be displaced by good goal images, never just driven out.

By burning into our minds the goals we picture, we can work toward success 24 hours a day, since that part of our brain does not sleep.

Make goals run your life by embodying them in an inner movie or TV script repeatedly played back in the mind. (p. 89)

By examining one's life, areas of strengths will be discovered that will bring satisfaction in being an acceptable human being. On the other hand, areas of weaknesses will be revealed that will need improvement. Redirecting goals will empower one to reverse negative aspects and change them into positive rewards. It is possible to become the person one wants to become by changing attitudes laden with feelings of disability to those with belief in the ability to achieve.

REDIRECTING GOALS WILL EMPOWER ONE TO REVERSE NEGATIVE ASPECTS AND CHANGE THEM INTO POSITIVE REWARDS

Lynne Bernfield's publication, *When You Can You Will*, offered food for thought that enables one to redirect goals to greater heights. She declared that goal directing is a process that comes from within. She issued these words of warning: "External success cannot heal internal wounds" (p. 190). She added that "before you love yourself, you must recognize that you're someone who deserves to be loved" (p. 200).

Included in Bernfield's advice for reaching greater heights are these ingredients for success for higher achievement:

Make your own list of pleasures and then allow yourself to experience them

Don't put off enjoying your life until it is what you think it should be

For just this moment accept yourself, as you are, because   you can't do what you can't do and WHEN YOU CAN YOU WILL. (p. 213)

Remember the magic of these words: When love is unconditional, it is a stupendous power for survival.

PROBLEM IDENTIFICATION

AND

PROBLEM SOLVING

WILL MAKE THE WEAK STRONG

AND

THE STRONG STRONGER

Chapter Four

FIND NEEDS
AND FILL THEM
TO ENRICH THE WORLD

Global needs are identified as deterrents to a world of peace, prosperity, and the personal development of all inhabitants on project Earth. A partial list of essential necessities to meet the needs of humanity, in our perception, includes these ten categories:

1. Health Services for All People
2. Family Stability
3. Quality Education for All Children
4. Parent Education and Involvement
5. Career Development Opportunities
6. Adequate Housing
7. Proper Nutrition

8. Spiritual Renewal
9. Economic Security
10. Peace in All Nations

Elaboration on the above perceived needs will justify our inclusion of each of them in the list. Filling each need will make the world suitable for all people to achieve their maximum potential.

1. HEALTH SERVICES FOR ALL PEOPLE

The current world status of health for children and families leaves much to be desired. Both preventive and corrective health services are needed for all people to develop and maintain healthy bodies. Too many families in the world are unable to get immunizations and other health care due to poverty and inaccessibility of health care institutions.

WHEN PEOPLE EXPERIENCE WELLNESS . . . PRODUCTIVITY SOARS AND THEIR SELF-ESTEEM IS ELEVATED

In third world countries health problems are magnified due to lack of human and material health resources. Health education programs are absent in many areas of the world. Lack of knowledge about preventive and corrective health practices results in numerous untimely and unnecessary deaths throughout the world.

Even in the United States, with its advanced medical technologies and state-of-the-art health facilities, there are crucial health problems among many underemployed and unemployed families who are unable to obtain health insurance coverage. National statistics reported in the *Times Dispatch,* September 29, 1998, stated that 43.4 million Americans had no health insurance in 1997. Of this number, 10.7 million were children. This is 15 percent of all American children.

Knowledge of the importance of good health was shared by the great Indian leader, Mahatma Ghandi, who said, "It is health which is real wealth and not pieces of gold and silver."

When people experience wellness and enjoy healthy bodies, their productivity soars and their self-esteem is elevated. Confirmation of this point of view can be found in the affirmation of Ralph Waldo Emerson when he said, "Give me health and a day, and I will make the pomp of emperors ridiculous."

2. FAMILY STABILITY

Unity of connection to a common ancestry and/or a succession of descendants of parents or parenting partners define a family. The stability of a family unit of related individuals—parents, children, and extended relations—represents soundness and steadiness in meeting challenges. Through mutual support, positive reinforcements, and unconditional love for each other as a permanent clan of relatives, family stability is ensured.

Since the beginning of biblical history, it has been observed that progress in family stability occurred when there was acceptance of heads of families as leaders. Traditions were passed on through instruction, role modeling, and the support of other people respected for their wisdom, knowledge, skills, and personal interest in enhancing excellence in their offspring.

THE STABILITY OF A FAMILY UNIT . . . REPRESENTS SOUNDNESS AND STEADINESS IN MEETING CHALLENGES

In biblical history, parents practiced family stability by teaching their children. They were mandated to "train a child in the way he should go and when he is old he will not depart from it." Human cultures have continued intact throughout generations through the use of informal education in the family.

3. QUALITY EDUCATION FOR ALL CHILDREN

Quality education is different from "schooling." Quality education draws out the best that is in an individual by providing a comprehensive exemplary program that develops the mind, body, and soul. While schooling is a process of instruction, it is not necessarily comprehensive in educating the "whole" child. In a society that enhances self-esteem, all children are challenged to soar like eagles, through the process of quality education, in order to achieve excellence in life's journey.

4. PARENT EDUCATION
AND INVOLVEMENT

Based on research conducted by Virgie M. Binford (1980), "parental involvement in the educational process is crucial as citizens are sometimes reluctant to support education because, in the opinion of some parents, schools are not responsive enough to the needs of students." This type of criticism is usually made when parents are not involved in the teaching/learning process.

Realizing that being a parent is not an automatic blueprint of assurance that home and school will work together to assist in reinforcing the learning experiences initiated in school, Dorothy N. Cowling founded the Library Home Project (1990), which provided both developmentally appropriate books for children to read in the home and "self-help" books for parents to improve their parenting strategies by enhancing their knowledge, skills, and creativity in strengthening home and family relationships. In addition to donating books, Cowling's project provided a

> PARENTAL INVOLVEMENT IN THE EDUCATIONAL PROCESS IS CRUCIAL AS CITIZENS ARE SOMETIMES RELUCTANT TO SUPPORT EDUCATION

mentorship component to share guidance and coun-
seling techniques as needed for children and families.

5. CAREER DEVELOPMENT OPPORTUNITIES

Faced with unemployment and underemploy-
ment in our technological society, families are in
need of training and retraining for securing jobs and
then maintaining the competencies
needed to hold onto employment.

KNOWLEDGE OF THE AVAILABILITY OF EMPLOYMENT OPPORTUNITY ENHANCES THE ESTEEM OF JOB SEEKERS

Knowledge of the availability of
employment opportunity enhances
the esteem of job seekers. Recognizing
that there are choices that can be
made to ensure the right person for
the right job in the right place
empowers them. Suggested lists of job
opportunities are shared in the
appendix as starter uppers for taking
advantage of career development
opportunities.

6. ADEQUATE HOUSING

The adage "there is no place like home" creates
a vision of a place where love and comfort are
present to provide feelings of peace and security.
Yet, many families are homeless. The self-esteem of
children is enormously injured when they attend
school and are unable to give a home address to

school personnel because they have none.

While there are many concerned, caring, and committed citizens trying to eliminate the housing problem through such programs as Habitat for Humanity and others, the demand for housing for the needy exceeds the available supply.

7. PROPER NUTRITION

A lack of balanced meals and an inadequate supply of food cause poor health and is evident in many families. Obesity in many children and families often results from improper diets with an overabundance of fatty foods and desserts.

High self-esteemers are able to secure proper nutritious foods. They know to combine good health habits of regular exercise and beneficial eating habits that set a lifetime pattern.

8. SPIRITUAL RENEWAL

The human heart longs for cleansing and wholeness of body. Daily meditation and/or prayer create "inner-winners" by renewing, revitalizing, restoring, and enriching the power and well-being of the soul, mind, and body. On the other hand, lack of spiritual renewal creates "outer-doubters," whose faith, hope, and unconditional love are diminished.

DAILY MEDITATION AND/OR PRAYER CREATE "INNER-WINNERS"

Lack of spiritual renewal leads to undue stress and improper time management. The outcome of spiritual renewal causes people to eliminate negative forces and accentuate the positive forces that increase self-esteem for inward strength to enhance success in all areas of life.

9. ECONOMIC SECURITY

The cliché "a penny saved is a penny earned" is true, but when pennies are not available, financial security and economic status are low. Individuals become powerless to gain economic security. Suggested remedies to overcome the disaster of families with inadequate or no income include providing job training and continuing instruction for success on the job. This commitment would promote economic security and propel self-esteem to a new height.

10. PEACE IN ALL NATIONS

Peace on Earth will be realized when each citizen resolves to be at peace in his or her actions and interactions. Recognizing that it takes at least two people to cause a disturbance, we can turn the quest for peace into reality through an unconditional love shared to bring about peaceful resolutions to all challenges. Goodwill to all mankind is a possibility when true brotherhood and sisterhood are engaged in amid all human behavioral circumstances.

PEACE ON EARTH WILL BE REALIZED WHEN EACH CITIZEN RESOLVES TO BE AT PEACE

The ongoing process of creating peace is strengthened through the affirmation of "let there be peace and let it begin with me." Seeing the good traits in everyone empowers each one of us to know the value of cultivating our spiritual gifts in order to harvest the fruits of the spirit. When we find universal human needs and fill them, there will be peace in all nations.

PLAN WITH HIGH EXPECTATIONS
FOR ACHIEVEMENTS

"WHATEVER YOU ASK FOR IN PRAYER
WITH FAITH, YOU WILL RECEIVE."
MATTHEW 21:22

Chapter Five

Expect the Best from Well-Made Plans

Well-made plans enable a person to climb each and every rung on the ladder of success and to reach new heights of attainment. Well-made plans fuel the fire of enthusiasm in goal setting and decision making.

Plans in every area of life signify that there is a purpose for living. They crystallize the aim for success in continuous achievement. Robert Browning suggested that "the aim, if reached or not, makes great the life."

Fidelity in planning revitalizes purposeful living and enhances the will to succeed in spite of the inevitable adversities and obstacles that place stumbling blocks in our pathway toward the achievement of our plans.

High expectations prime the pump of planning by preparing us to achieve our visions of faith, hope, and unconditional love of all mankind. They are the seeds of the fruit of one's labors and the roots of survival for mastery of one's fate.

History is crowded with high achievers who expected the best from well-made plans. People in bondages such as slavery envisioned being free and struggled to make their fondest dreams come true.

Examples of these forward-moving souls include Harriet Tubman, who dared to risk her life and the pursuit of her own happiness by helping her family and friends escape to freedom. As the conductor of the "Underground Railroad," she expected the best from her plans.

HISTORY IS CROWDED WITH HIGH ACHIEVERS WHO EXPECTED THE BEST FROM WELL-MADE PLANS

Mahatma Gandhi expected the best from his inner self and expressed his views to convert others to his positive thoughts. He said, "Each one has to find his peace from within, and peace to be real must be unaffected by outside circumstances."

An idea for expecting the best of well-made plans was shared by Martin Luther King Jr. in these words: "We must use time wisely and forever realize that the time is always ripe to do what is right."

Physical handicaps will not deter success when there is a system of belief surrounding one's determination to achieve. To illuminate this, Helen Keller overcame the twin afflictions of blindness and deafness to affirm that "nothing can be done without hope and confidence." She also said, "We can do anything if we stick to it long enough."

Expectations are the dreams of winners in life. Harry Kemp verified this belief with this statement: "The poor man is not he who is without a cent, but he who is without a dream."

Expecting the best has its rewards in achievement. This point

> EXPECTATIONS ARE THE DREAMS OF WINNERS IN LIFE. . . . EXPECTING THE BEST HAS ITS REWARDS IN ACHIEVEMENT

of view was expounded on by Thomas Edison in these words: "If we did all the things we are capable of doing, we would literally astound ourselves."

When we expect the best of self and others we will have "spin-off" benefits that promote peace, harmony, and greatness. In the words of John Steinbeck: "It is the nature of man to rise to greatness if greatness is expected of him."

In the authors' years of involvement in the teaching/learning process from preschool to university levels, we have observed students whose life chances for success were minimal. However, with seeds of self-confidence planted within their hearts, minds, and souls, they overcame obstacles of hopelessness, developed "I can" attitudes, and made significant strides to achieve greatness in many areas of life.

GUIDELINES FOR
ACHIEVING BEST PLANS

Accept things you are unable to modify in daily living.

Communicate your needs to your Higher Power.

Have alternate plans that may be used as substitutes.

Invite mentors to give you their support in your planning.

Exchange points of view and prioritize them in order of preferences.

Visualize success in all of the plans you make.

Inspire enthusiasm by utilizing positive affirmations.

Nurture successful ventures with sincere, honest praise.

Grade your progress with Good, Better, and Best ratings.

Be alert, concerned, caring, and committed to developing plans and strategies and achieving them with support of trusting mentors.

Expect positive results from all plans. Make entries into a journal of actions and inter-actions that worked in the process of planning and implementing plans.

Sacrifice time to share gratitude to all who assisted you in developing, implementing, and monitoring your action plans.

Talk with people who know as much or more than you do to obtain assistance in achieving well-made plans.

Praise self and others for support and assis-tance in generating strategies for imple-menting defined plans that will make the world a better place.

Love all people unconditionally and expect quality performance from all of the people on your action team.

Accentuate positive strides toward the journey of success in making and achieving success with well-made plans.

Network with diversified groups and individuals to ensure a variety of sources of knowledge, skills, and creativity in making and implementing plans.

Share your accomplishments with others in an attitude of gratitude for jobs well-done.

ALWAYS EXPECT TO
OVERCOME OBSTACLES

Stories of the authors' pathways to the achievement of several milestones tell of overcoming adversities of poverty and inequality of opportunities because of the color of our skin and the barrenness of our physical environments. Yet, we were given positive reinforcement by family members, teachers, and friends. They inspired us to develop inner-winning spirits of high expectations in making contributions to help others achieve. We made continuous progress by expecting the best from well-made plans that enhanced our self-esteem.

WE MADE CONTINUOUS PROGRESS BY EXPECTING THE BEST FROM WELL-MADE PLANS THAT ENHANCED OUR SELF-ESTEEM

Our greatest rewards have been received when we meet former students who remind us of something we said or did that empowered them to elevate their expectations and make plans to pursue goals that encompassed positive outcomes for success.

Role models in our educational journey have been numerous. We still utilize the interdependence of sharing and caring as we plan, implement, and monitor our actions in crystallizing our aims for making the world a better place.

Our unconditional love for all people frees us to become both goal- and people-oriented and to expect the best from well-made plans.Over a half century of studying, learning, teaching, and being taught through firsthand and vicarious enriching experiences, we have crystallized our beliefs to affirm that *all people can learn.*

WE WERE GIVEN POSITIVE REINFORCEMENT BY FAMILY MEMBERS, TEACHERS, AND FRIENDS

We firmly believe that doors of opportunity are opened through caring attitudes, undauntable faith in self and a Higher Power, and that unconditional love for all people will ignite sparks of hope in the hopeless, immeasurable joy in joyless souls and self-sufficient confidence in low or negative self-esteemers.

Life's journey filled with enhancement of dreams, goals, and determination to succeed, in spite of handicapping conditions, can result in smooth travel when one is surrounded by positive travellers with commonalities of purpose. Teams of self-esteem enhancers will generate openness of spirit and will share cloaks of nurture and reinforcement for achieving desired outcomes.

Our diversified experiences in many institutions of learning involving thousands of students and hosts of global reinforcers proved that "in unity there is strength in goal setting and decision making to overcome obstacles in life."

AFFIRMATION

"God is our refuge and strength,
a very present help in time of trouble."
PSALM 46:1

Chapter Six

SEEK DIVINE GUIDANCE IN EVERYTHING YOU THINK, SAY, AND DO

 The thoughts, images, and perceptions that cross upon the screens of your mind become the blueprint you will use to build your future. The Bible says, "As a man thinketh in his heart, so is he" (Prov. 23:7 KJV).

Instead of saying, "I cannot believe," you can believe. "I can do all things through Christ who strengthens me." When you change your way of thinking, it will change your actions.

- You must give your very life to becoming and developing a positive disposition.
- Act better than you feel.
- Cut your line when it is tangled.

- Keep cool, even when you are angry.
- Make your relationship right.

To seek divine guidance in everything you do, you have to have faith in yourself and God.

The first step in putting misfortune or negativism in proper perspective is to confront the unpleasant side of life squarely and accept it as a fact of life. If you take the attitude that things will not always go well or as planned, you will be especially happy and thankful when they do go well, and you will avoid dismay when they do not go as you had hoped.

This attitude will help you become a realist, not a pessimist, and you will be better prepared to capitalize on negative and failed events. "Attitudes are more important than facts," said Karl Menninger. Dr. Paul Faulkner showed that the key to happiness rests in mastering our attitude. All that we are and all that we do are products of our attitudes about life. Psychological tests reveal that our responses toward others are determined more by our attitudes than by what others actually do.

ALL THAT WE ARE AND ALL THAT WE DO ARE PRODUCTS OF OUR ATTITUDES ABOUT LIFE

I was quite young when I first heard the Biblical passage, "As a man thinketh, so is he." Little did I understand that the Biblical passage had hit the nail of truth squarely on the head. In the last two decades scientists (and I) have learned more about the workings of the human brain than was known throughout all history prior to that time. I now know that by an incredibly complex physiological mechanism, a joint effort of body, brain, and "mind," we become the living result of our own thoughts. Through scientific discovery, we have proved the relationship between our own "mental programming" and the success or failure of any endeavor we undertake in life, from something as important as a lifetime goal to something as small as what we do in a single day.

IT IS VIRTUALLY IMPOSSIBLE FOR ANY OF US TO DO ANYTHING, NO MATTER HOW INSIGNIFICANT, WITHOUT BEING AFFECTED BY OUR CONDITIONING

Authorities say what you do, how you act, and how successful you become are dependent on the conditioning and programming you received from others and on the conditioning you subsequently keep giving yourself. It is virtually impossible for any of us to do anything, no matter how insignificant, without being affected by our conditioning.

Therefore, it follows that if every action you take, of any kind, is affected by prior programming, then the end results of your actions are equally affected. After examining the philosophies, the theories, and the practiced methods of influencing human behavior, you will become what you think about most. Your success or failure in anything, large or small, will depend on your programming and what you accept from others.

It is up to each of us to change our life. It is up to each of us to make things right when things go wrong. And God has given us the power to do so. The mandate to seek divine guidance in everything we think, say, and do must be evidenced in our performance.

Relying on a power that is greater than self will enable one to soar to new heights in every area of life. On the eve of a new millenium, with so many challenges in life, it is necessary to have a higher power to guide one's growth and development in all actions and interactions.

During daily tasks a diversity of activities often places undue pressure on individuals, families, and groups trying to cope with adversities that strain bodies, minds, and souls. Relief can be discovered when connections are made to ease the weighty challenges that shackle peaceful existence in environments laden with turmoil.

RELYING ON A POWER THAT IS GREATER THAN SELF WILL ENABLE ONE TO SOAR TO NEW HEIGHTS IN EVERY AREA OF LIFE

Divine guidance is within reach of all who are willing to submit to acquisition of inner peace through prayer or meditation. Numerous volumes are published on the power of releasing pent-up emotions and centering self on positive thoughts through communication. An atmosphere of quietness and an emptiness of useless baggage of mind clutterers are necessary to eliminate heavily laden pressures that cause unrest and distress.

Creative visualization in the stillness of one's peaceful environment opens the floodgate of thoughts that center mind, body, and soul on peaceful scenes, enhancing tranquility of the spirit. Divine guidance also reveals possibilities for coping with situations that may have caused undue stress in the past.

DIVINE GUIDANCE IS WITHIN REACH OF ALL THROUGH PRAYER OR MEDITATION

Staying focused on one's cherished affirmations will empower creative visualization to work faster than if there is no guiding phrase or verse to promote divine guidance in the process. Some people engaged in creative visualization or in contemplative prayer choose to silently affirm a favorite Bible verse or a positive affirmation that fulfills an "as if" principle. This approach feeds the mind and soul with a thought or an expression that has already happened in one's life.

Action plans should follow a quiet session of visualization or contemplative prayer to crystallize and actualize the ideas that were created during the period of meditation. Objectives should be listed in a journal with a time frame as a guide for the achievement of these goals and fondest dreams.

Daily pursuits of steps toward the accomplishments of one's goals will keep inspiration active and hope alive with an abundance of faith for continuous success.

Testimonies in the autobiographies and biographies of many successful people illustrate that in the midst of turmoil and obstacles that would cause many people to give up on the achievement of their desired goals, they kept the faith by maintaining an "as if" principle uppermost in their visions.

THE "AS IF" PRINCIPLE

The following are some examples of "as if" thoughts:

- I am healthy, happy, and terrific.

- I can do all things through Christ who strengthens me.

- I have adequate financial resources to meet my needs.

- I am organized, productive, and soar as a high achiever in every area of life.

Other phrases or sentences may be used, tailored to meet the unique needs and specific interests of the visualizers.

Guidelines that help to utilize divine guidance include this daily living action program:

- Share daily gratitude for achieving progress in every component of life—no matter how small the positive results may be.

- Praise those whose support you shared and those who spoke words of encouragement to you.

- Thank those who demonstrated acceptance of your objectives as valid for improving quality of life for self and others.

- Keep a journal for writing ideas, a plan of action, and daily success stories.

- Maintain specificity in recording entries in the daily journal.

- Share with others why the act of gratitude is important to you.

- Write steps you plan to take to realize continuous improvement.

- Write personal notes to those who helped you become open to divine guidance.

Model What You Learn
to
Enhance Competencies
as an
Effective Teacher

"Teaching is to awaken joy
in creative expression."

Albert Einstein

Chapter Seven

TEACH WHAT YOU LEARN TO INCREASE THE EXPLOSION OF KNOWLEDGE

 Enhancing excellence in education depends on the multiplication of knowledge, skills, and creativity through sharing and reinforcing what is known with those who need to improve. The primary responsibility in teaching is to assume leadership to bring out the best in others. It has been said that "leaders must know where they are going and must be able to take others with them." To teach, then, is to lead others to utilize their human potential.

Those in various careers who have made significant contributions in the teaching/learning process used positive actions to concentrate on the worthy aspects of living and learning and replicated them on a wide basis for improvement of the total population. They were mentored by someone and they in turn mentored others, thus increasing the explosion of knowledge. This snowball effect increased the positive actions of many people.

The authors of this publication are prime examples of the positive effects of the ever-increasing mentorship program. We were blessed to have had mentors in many areas of life including career development. Both of us recall caring, concerned, and committed teachers who gave us faith in ourselves, hope for a brighter future in our careers, and unconditional love along the way. These mentors were people who were not only certified as teachers, but who also used wisdom and spiritual guidance to give us positive reinforcement.

PROVIDING INNER-WINNING EXPERTISE TO EMPOWER MENTEES IS AN IMPORTANT GOAL

Through the years we have strived to make concerted efforts to mentor others, including children and families with whom we have interacted in curricular and extracurricular activities. Results of our efforts have been evidenced in seeing our mentees grow and develop and become mentors to others.

Building a trusting relationship with others and helping them to find needs and fill them are primary responsibilities of mentors to mentees. Providing inner-winning expertise to empower mentees in the following areas is an important goal for the mentor/mentee relationship:

- self-acceptance
- self-respect
- self-control
- self-confidence
- self-worth

Assisting mentees to develop wholeness in mind, body, and soul is important in the job description of mentors. These areas add to the effectiveness of the teaching/learning process:

- physical fitness
- intellectual development
- home and family relationships
- spiritual and ethical values
- social and cultural development
- financial management

When there is an effective match between mentors and mentees the teaching/learning process will be reciprocal—each will teach and each will learn.

The authors' interaction as mentor and mentee crisscross. For several decades we have been guided by the utilization of personal strengths in the process of growth and development. We began the teaching/learning process as school administrator and student intern. Dr. Cowling was the principal of the laboratory school where I, Dr. Binford, was assigned

EACH WILL TEACH AND EACH WILL LEARN

to do my undergraduate internship. She initiated an informal program of guidance and positive reinforcement as a mentor for all of her practice teachers. Concerted efforts were made to draw out the maximum potential of each person. Her only reward was her mandate for us to replicate the services she provided for needy persons. Years later, after earning bachelor's and master's degrees, I was honored to be employed as an adjunct instructor at Virginia Union University in teacher education while I worked as an educator for the Richmond public schools. Dr. Cowling's continuous mentorship provided positive reinforcement for me while she served as an educational consultant, proposal writer, and supervisor of instructional practices for professionals, paraprofessionals, parents, and students.

Our mentor/mentee relationship continued to be activated in several professional and civic organizations. We worked with groups from diversified backgrounds and cultures to grow and develop as a team of caring, concerned, and committed teachers and learners. One of Dr. Cowling's favorite mandates was, "We must continue to stretch our minds and spiritual gifts to new horizons in order to bring out the best in others." She also stated, and demonstrated in numerous ways, that success is continuous and must be cultivated on a daily basis.

> SUCCESS IS CONTINUOUS AND MUST BE CULTIVATED ON A DAILY BASIS

A TEACH AND LEARN RECIPE

Take time to teach others what you know.

Expect the best from everyone you meet.

Accept every person as a biological wonder.

Communicate faith, hope, and love with everyone.

Hear all sides of a discussion before drawing a conclusion.

Act "as if" you are an outstanding teacher and learner and it will always be a reality.

Network to grow and develop strengths.

Devote time to think, to do, and to act responsibly.

Love unconditionally all people.

Energize yourself to be enthusiastic about the importance of the teaching/learning process.

Assist the needy without expectation of a reward.

Revitalize yourself to reinforce others to excel.

Nurture the good in all people and eliminate their shortcomings.

Utilizing this recipe, we remind listeners of the importance of preparation for excellence. We make conscious efforts to choose to be the best by preparing, practicing, and building on foundations of excellence that were laid by mentors. It was their shoulders that we stood on that empowered us to carve opportunities out of adversities and turn the lemons in life into lemonades of appreciation. The powerful attributes of faith, hope, and love that they taught us must be passed on to others.

ENERGIZE YOUR LIFE
AND
REDIRECT GOALS
TO
REACH GREATER HEIGHTS

Chapter Eight

EXAMINE YOUR LIFE AND REDIRECT GOALS TO REACH GREATER HEIGHTS

 Advocators of improvement in all areas of life are in agreement that "the greatest room is the room for improvement." This challenge is accepted by us and is passed on in our daily actions as we search for ways to grow and develop our hidden talents in order to be of greater service to all mankind.

Elevating ideas for helping others to develop their maximum potential by improving our knowledge, skills, and creative actions must be ongoing. We, therefore, have redirected our energies from a goal of earning money to providing humanitarian services for the needy.

Recognizing the value of reading as a tool for reaching greater heights in life, Dr. Cowling founded a home library for needy children and families. Her goal was simple—to establish a love for reading. This opened doors of understanding and developed appreciation for the communicative arts as methods for achieving greater heights in life. With the assistance of a small committee of caring, concerned, and committed members of the Virginia Area Chapter of Pi Lambda Theta, an international honor society in education, the dream of this project became a reality; after several years of operation, the project expanded from serving a selected area to the metropolitan area of Richmond, Virginia. Procedures for the success of this project include recruiting interested families; providing workshops in developmental, functional, and recreational reading; and selecting developmentally appropriate reading materials for all members in selected families. Significant gains are evidenced in both the cognitive and affective domains of participants.

> HER GOAL WAS SIMPLE—TO ESTABLISH A LOVE FOR READING

The spirit of Dr. Cowling's efforts to initiate the home library project has ignited other interested groups and is being replicated on a wider basis.

Feedback from parents and children indicates that the home library project is enhancing school achievement and career development. It is also serving as a deterrent to boredom. Having interesting books to read as a supplement to schoolwork eliminates the statement of "I have nothing to do after schoolwork."

Subscribing to the adage that "an idle mind is the devil's workshop" propelled the growth of the home library to a higher dimension of priority in goal setting and in decision making of families.

Sharing books as rewards for those who have found success in school by modifying their behavior from reluctance to interest in reading keeps the project alive. It is gratifying to note that more and more children and families are being rewarded for their efforts in taking steps to improve by making reading fun.

Proponents of the home library project believe that we will become a nation of literates if we continue to concentrate on changing one family at a time. We further believe that it takes the concerted efforts of all to pass the torch of mastery of the communicative arts to home, school, and community. Making learning fun and fundamental in families enhances success in developing wholeness in the teaching/learning process.

MAKING LEARNING FUN AND FUNDAMENTAL IN FAMILIES ENHANCES SUCCESS

By examining our personal lives and redirecting our goals and objectives to sharing our resources with the less fortunate, we will forge ahead in helping others to climb the ladder of success. Then, we must reach back and pull others along as we continue to find needs and fill them in a campaign to promote a library in every home.

CHARACTERISTICS OF
INNER-WINNERS

I nvite others to emulate their acceptable behavior in all situations.

N urture seeds of greatness that are present in all people.

N etwork with "winners" to promote growth and development.

E nergize themselves to keep focused on continuous progress in goal setting and decision making.

R eact with positive thinking and actions in all situations.

Work diligently and consistently to improve self and others.

Inspire others to join them to form a larger team of willing workers.

Notice areas of need exhibited by people, places, and things and fill them.

Needle reluctant people, in the spirit of unconditional love, to join the team of inner-winners.

Expect positive results every time from diligent workers.

Reward progress with special celebrations of success.

Share good news of winning teams with diversified audiences.

Life's journey can be made tolerable with increments of success provided by a team of inner-winners who believe in the importance of developing the human potential of all people. As mentioned in earlier chapters, those of us who succeeded in achieving our goals were empowered by a team of people. They shared their time and talents to move us along the pathway of success. It is our responsibility to keep the engine of success fueled and in excellent running condition. We are determined to add coaches full of travelers and carry the travelers to a destination of self-fulfillment. They, in turn, must be coaxed into recruiting others and replicate services in the inner-winning business.

IT IS OUR RESPONSIBILITY TO KEEP THE ENGINE OF SUCCESS FUELED AND IN EXCELLENT RUNNING CONDITION

Providing leadership training for others to take our places and soar like eagles in their respective careers will keep the pathway of success illuminated with willing inner-winners. It is not enough for a few renowned leaders to assume their rightful places at the wheel of life. They are saddled with the responsibility of keeping the wheel of life rolling with additional spokes to speed up the movement toward improvement in every component of daily living.

Our observation in volunteer work with a group of teenagers in leadership development is that, with tender loving care and high expectations, they are excelling in planning and implementing programs that benefit others with greater needs than themselves. With the support of families and other care takers, they are graciously accepting advice and are utilizing their time and talents to serve as leaders for younger children in home, school, and community activities.

These teenagers demonstrate belief in the affirmation that "whatever the mind can conceive and believe, by the grace of our Creator, we can achieve."

As goodwill ambassadors, we must take the helm of leadership. We must prove that we will share with and care for others as we demonstrate the "why" and "how" of being enablers for others to follow in our footsteps.

With special efforts, the journey of success becomes a circle of faith, hope, and love. When people join hands, hearts, minds, bodies, and souls with determination, when their desires, dreams, daring spirits, prayers, and praise join together in a mission of kindness and acts of gratitude, progress is assured. Numbers of trustworthy and determined winners will multiply and join the race of those who put the development of the human potential of others as a priority.

Encouragement on a continuous basis, along with positive reinforcement, enhance the capability and inspiration of others. This rippling stream of progress widens the circle of leaders and followers and keeps the upward mobility of all people soaring to newer heights of accomplishments in every area of life.

GUIDELINES
FOR
EFFECTIVE
SELF-ESTEEM ENHANCERS

Chapter Nine

SELF-ESTEEM ENHANCERS

A wise quotation by an unknown author, "What you do speaks so loudly, I cannot hear a word you say," is applicable to the need of role models to demonstrate moral and spiritual values as guidelines for success in life.

Our mission is to show how to make wise choices in discerning right from wrong. We are obligated to share ways in which all of us can profit from mistakes made by self and others. Yet, we must refrain from criticizing, condemning, and complaining about situations when we possess inadequate information to objectively prove a point of view.

Based upon the Holy Bible's mandate, we must practice forgiveness and "be kind to one another,

Make preparation to succeed by communicating excellence in everything you say and do.

Organize thoughts and actions to present a model of an exemplary person in all areas of life.

Devote time for meditation and contemplative prayer.

Energize self daily with an "I Can" attitude of willingness to work for self-improvement.

Love others as well as yourself unconditionally.

Be ready to accept challenges to speak the truth in all situations.

Elevate opportunities through continuous study and application of what is learned.

Help others to overcome obstacles in life without expectation of rewards.

Avoid arguments and interactions with people who frustrate the spirit.

Vitalize your personal life, workplace, and community with positive attributes of peace, harmony, and beauty.

Instill in self and others dreams and opportunities to excel as contributors of resources to make the world a better place.

Open the doors of understanding to the importance of peacekeeping and harmony in audiences of multicultural/multiethnic groups.

Respect all people and give sincere, honest praise lavishly.

tenderhearted, forgiving each other, just as God in Christ has forgiven you" (Eph. 4:32).

With peace in our hearts, and with clarity of purpose for advocating moral and spiritual development, we can model desirable behavior at all times.

MODEL BEHAVIOR

Guidelines for demonstrating model behavior are reminders that (1) in order to cope with challenges in life one must always make right choices, and (2) in order to survive one must always be a respectable citizen in our society.

The positive outcome of model behavior will attract others with the desire and determination to emulate similar characteristics. Thus, the seeds of spiritual development will sprout and flourish to actualize an abundance of faith, hope, and love that will widen like a rippling stream in society.

Enhancers in self-esteem development are numerous. They include involvement of mind, body, soul, and inner strength to ensure acquisition of coping skills on a journey of peace, pleasure, positive thoughts, and actions in the achievement of fondest dreams. The partnerships of favorable thoughts and actions eliminate negative forces and cultivate positive strides toward the actualization of

THE SEEDS OF SPIRITUAL DEVELOPMENT WILL SPROUT AND FLOURISH TO ACTUALIZE AN ABUNDANCE OF FAITH, HOPE, AND LOVE

desired end results. They result in significant increases of faith, hope, and unconditional love for self and all mankind.

Summarizing our beliefs and those of numerous high self-esteemers, we capsuled our views in these "power points" of food for thought:

S earch for truth in everything you say and do in order to survive as "sellers" of the best possible solutions to any of life's challenges that hamper progress.

E nable others to join a team of positive thinkers to enlarge the circle of those who are dedicated to finding needs and filling them in order to make the world a desirable place to reside in with goodwill towards all mankind.

L ove animate and inanimate beings and things as a catharsis for cleansing of stressful thoughts and demon-related actions. Learn to appreciate the goodness of all inhabitants on project Earth.

F oster peace through helping hands and grateful hearts that are focused on lifting others up to climb the ladder of success.

E xchange ideas for strengthening the goals and objectives of those who put forth every conceivable effort to improve on esteeming actions that are worthy of replication on a wider scale.

S avor hopes and dreams of achievement in the development of a framework of stepping stones to the elevation of visions of limitless success.

T rample feelings of doubt and dismay with power-driven tools of compassion and development of tested strategies that erase fear of survival in all situations.

E xamine self and remove all obstructions that cloud the belief system of self-worth and self-acceptance.

E xpress genuine affection for all human beings in daily communication at home, the workplace, institutions of teaching and learning, and in extracurricular activities that are designed to enhance self-esteem.

M ake opportunities for personal growth and for the growth of others in all actions and interactions.

E xplain views in loving ways that will convince others of the value of affirming benefits of healthy actions toward self and others.

N urture thoughts for exploring possibilities for the improvement of ideas for successful ventures in journeys of faith.

H arness spiritual-enriching techniques for building and enhancing self-esteem to empower self and others to succeed as inner-winners.

A ccept ideas as starter-uppers for generating a storehouse of techniques for improvement in all areas of life.

N etwork with positive people who are engaged in upward mobility in physical, intellectual, social, emotional, and spiritual growth.

C ommit to continuous progress and improve everyday with affirmations that will enhance growth and development.

E ntertain a circle of positive thinking team members on a regular basis for ongoing planning, implementing, and monitoring of success-oriented strategies.

R evitalize self and others with positive reinforcement of words and deeds that will foster and stimulate motivation.

S hare success stories to spread the good news of the power of thinking and believing in the attributes of healthy self-esteem in the enhancement of the quality of life. Pursue happiness in an "as if" attitude to ensure a safe and secure journey on the road to fulfillment of desires.

We conclude that healthy self-esteem is a builder of the best qualities in individuals. It opens doors of understanding that success is a journey of faith in a Supreme Being, hope for a brighter future, and unconditional love for everyone. These enhancers to life will add quality to survival on project Earth.

MODEL BEHAVIOR IS ONGOING AND NEEDS TO BE PRACTICED DAILY FOR SUCCESS

Model behavior is not a onetime development. It is ongoing and needs to be practiced daily for success.

Prayer and meditation must be accompanied by concerted actions of unconditional love for self and others. Finding needs and filling them will accelerate the process of building a structure of incontestable values for the realization of enhancers for healthy self-esteem.

Trustworthy teams of positive thinkers and actors should be recruited to organize a support system for continuous planning, implementing, and evaluating progress in developing programs to improve every aspect of life.

REFLECTING ON THE PAST

EXPERIENCING THE PRESENT

AND

PREDICTING THE FUTURE

Chapter Ten

TEN KEYS OF SELF-ESTEEM

 Our goals and objectives in this publication were anchored around our perception of Self-Esteem Enhancers. Strength-building structures of strategies that have worked for us and thousands of others were shared.

Interactions with groups and individuals from diversified backgrounds in the past convinced us that successful ideas for developing self-acceptance, self-respect, self-control, self-confidence, and self-worth should be replicated. The achievement of objectives to produce healthy bodies, minds, and souls in the teaching/learning process inspired us to write this book.

Key concepts utilized in the past are still working for us in various settings that include multicultural/

AN ACRONYM FOR SELF-ESTEEM

S earch for ideas to stimulate interest in self-improvement.

E nergize your life with positive affirmations.

L ove self and others unconditionally.

F ind needs and fill them to enrich the world.

E xpect the best from well-made plans.

S eek divine guidance in everything you think, say, and do.

T each what you learn to increase the explosion of knowledge about positive actions of people.

E xamine your life and redirect goals to reach greater heights.

E ncourage everyone you meet to join the team of inner-winners.

M odel behavior to demonstrate faith, hope, and love in moral and spiritual development.

multiethnic groups in homes, schools, workplaces, and community settings.

Presently, we are staying involved in sharing our knowledge, skills, and creativity in self-esteem enhancing activities locally, nationally, and internationally with various ages from children to retired persons. Inner-winning spirits of joy and self-fulfillment reward us when we see positive results from our efforts.

Whether we are working as educational consultants or volunteering in a variety of projects, our satisfaction comes from knowing that we are sharing and caring in areas of need.

As we face the new millennium, we predict that there will always be a need for self-enhancing programs that will provide coping skills to meet challenges in all areas of life. Hopefully, the ideas shared in this publication will serve as starter uppers to enhance the self-esteem of all readers and will stimulate others to add their knowledge to make our world a better place.

INCREASE AFFIRMATION ACTION

AND

DECREASE NEGATIVE CRITICISM

TO

ACCELERATE FAITH, HOPE,

AND

UNCONDITIONAL LOVE

Appendix A

ABCs OF SELF-ESTEEM

 Self-esteem enhancers have proven to be effective. We have used these principles in workshops conducted for diversified groups in numerous places that included multicultural/multiethnic participants.

As teachers and learners, we developed a "handout" of guidelines utilizing the alphabet. This invaluable tool is one that may be used for crystal-lizing knowledge, skills, and creativity for reinforcing ideas we shared in various sessions. We include these tested messages of faith, hope, and unconditional love with the expectation that the results will be evident.

ABCs of

Accept yourself.

Believe in your potential.

Commit yourself to excellence.

Dare to dream big dreams.

Engage in daily study.

Find needs and fill them.

Give your service to others.

Help the less fortunate.

Involve mind, body, and soul.

Join a team of positive thinkers.

Keep records of your success stories.

Love all people.

Make plans and implement them.

SELF-ESTEEM

Network for success.

Obey good health rules.

Put enthusiasm into your work.

Quit criticizing, condemning, and complaining.

Respond to opportunities with zest.

Seek goals to elevate your self-esteem.

Take time to think.

Understand self and improve.

Visualize success.

Work on prioritizing activities.

X-ray yourself to accentuate positive actions.

Yearn for contentment and make it happen.

Zap all obstacles and make them opportunities.

"A good education consists in giving
to the body and the soul
all the beauty and all the perfection
of which they are capable."

PLATO

Appendix B

SELF-ESTEEM JOURNAL

Daily entries in a self-esteem building journal will keep one focused on continuous self-improvement. Utilize creative visualization with simple sentences or phrases in the present tense. Some examples are:

—I am demonstrating my capability of achieving my
goal to _____ (be specific).
—I am verifying daily progress toward achieving my
goal by _____ (be specific).

Choose a specific time and place to write in your journal every day. Choose a mentor you trust with whom to share your entries for objective feedback. Add pages as needed.

A ccept yourself._____
_____
_____
_____

B elieve in your potential._____
_____
_____
_____

C ommit yourself to excellence. _____
_____
_____
_____

D are to dream big dreams. _____
_____
_____
_____

E ngage in daily study. _____
_____
_____
_____

F ind needs and fill them. _____
_____
_____
_____

G ive your service to others. _____
_____
_____
_____

Help the less fortunate._____
_____
_____
_____

Involve mind, body, and soul. _____
_____
_____
_____

Join a team of positive thinkers. _____
_____
_____
_____

Keep records of your success stories._____
_____
_____
_____

Love all people. _____
_____
_____
_____

Make plans and implement them. _____
_____
_____
_____

Network for success. _____
_____
_____
_____

Obey good health rules. _____

_____

_____

_____

Put enthusiasm into your work. _____

_____

_____

_____

Quit criticizing, condemning, and complaining. ___

_____

_____

_____

Respond to opportunities with zest. _____

_____

_____

_____

Seek goals to elevate your self-esteem. _____

_____

_____

_____

Take time to think. _____

_____

_____

Understand self and improve. _____

_____

_____

_____

Visualize success. _____

_____

_____

_____

Work on prioritizing activities. _____

_____

_____

_____

X-ray yourself to accentuate positive actions. _____

_____

_____

_____

Yearn for contentment and make it happen. _____

_____

_____

_____

Zap all obstacles and make them opportunities. ____

_____

_____

_____

BIBLIOGRAPHY

Beattie, Melody. *Codependent No More*. New York: Harper, 1987.

Bernfield, Lynne. *When You Can You Will*. Chicago: Contemporary Books, 1993.

Buscaglia, Leo. *Bus 9 To Paradise*. New York: William Morrow & Co., 1986.

Cepacchione, Lucia. *Recovery of Your Inner Child*. New York: Simon & Schuster, 1991.

Covey, Stephen. *Principle Centered Leadership*. New York: Summit Books, 1991.

Dyer, Wayne. *You'll See It When You Believe It*. New York: William Morrow, 1989.

———. *Your Erroneous Zones*. New York: Funk & Wagnalls, 1983.

————. *The Sky's the Limit*. New York: Simon & Schuster, 1980.

Gawain, Shakti. *Creative Visualization Workbook*. San Rafael, Calif.: New World Library, 1995.

Holy Bible (NIV). Grand Rapids, Mich.: Zondervan Pub. Co., 1984.

Kaiser, Stearns. *Living through Job Loss*. New York: Simon & Schuster, 1995.

Leman, Kevin. *Bringing Up Kids without Tearing Them Down*. New York: Bantam, Doubleday, 1993.

Linkletter, Art. *Yes You Can—How to Succeed in Business*. New York: Simon & Schuster, 1979.

London, Kathleen. *Who Am I? Who Are You?* Reading, Mass.: Addison-Wesley, 1995.

Steinem, Gloria. *Revolution from Within: A Book of Self-Esteem*. Boston: Little, Brown & Co., 1992.